BECOMING
A GREAT
GOD
PARENT

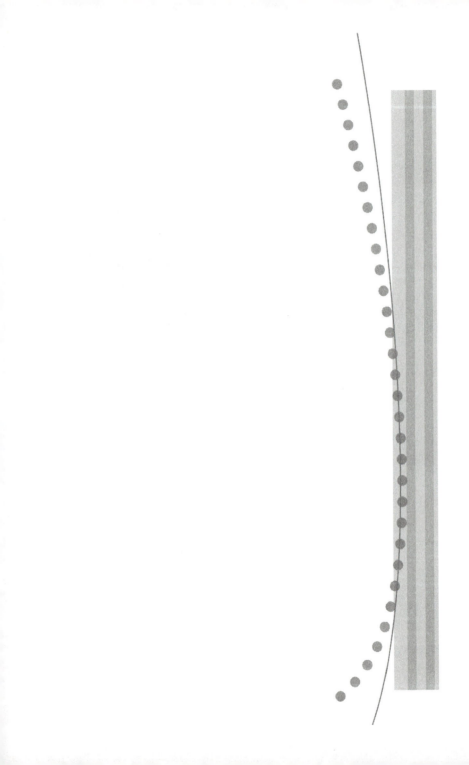

EVERYTHING A CATHOLIC
NEEDS TO KNOW

BECOMING
A GREAT
GOD
PARENT

PARACLETE PRESS
BREWSTER, MASSACHUSETTS

2013 First Printing

Becoming a Great Godparent: Everything a Catholic Needs to Know

Copyright © 2013 by Paraclete Press, Inc.

ISBN: 978-1-61261-363-5

Library of Congress Cataloging-in-Publication Data

Becoming a great godparent : everything a Catholic needs to know.
    pages cm
  ISBN 978-1-61261-363-5
  1. Sponsors. I. Paraclete Press.
  BV1478.B43 2013
  248.8'45—dc23   2012048232

10 9 8 7 6 5 4 3 2 1

Published by Paraclete Press
Brewster, Massachusetts
www.paracletepress.com

Printed in the United States of America

Dedicated to
every godparent
who joyfully
accepts these
enormous
responsibilities.

"Train children in the right way,

and when old, they will not stray."

–Proverbs 22:6

Presented to

_____

Godparent(s) to

_____

On This Date

_____

Thank you for being my godparents.

I am glad you will be walking

beside me, to love and to guide me.

I thank God I have godparents chosen with love.

CONTENTS

BECOMING
A GREAT
GOD
PARENT

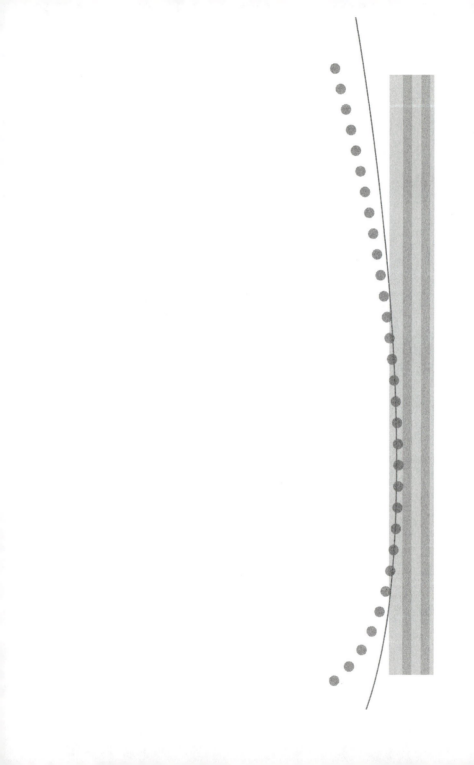

CHAPTER ONE

What Does a Great Godparent Do?

This is perhaps the first question that popped into your mind when you were asked to consider being a godparent for the first time:

What would I do?

You are definitely being asked to do some important things in the life of this child. This isn't a one-time thing. Being a godparent is more than attending a Baptism or purchasing a gift. It involves a lot more than being good friends with the child's parents. Your friends or relatives—the ones who asked you to play this important role in the life of their child—have invited you to be as close as family for their son or daughter, and to help them, and the child, by doing some very specific things for decades to come.

Are you ready?

This is a great honor. And clearly you aren't taking it lightly. That's why you are here, reading this book. So, let's summarize what great godparents do.

In a nutshell, great godparents are those who are:

Physically present as sponsors, and thoughtfully and prayerfully involved on the occasion of the child's Baptism; and then later, for his or her Confirmation.

● ● ● ● ●

Physically present at other important moments in the child's life as he or she grows into adulthood. If the child lives nearby, this is simple. But even if he or she lives far away, godparents need to make an effort to see the child frequently.

There to help guide the spiritual
formation and religious education of
the child.

● ● ● ● ●

Prepared to step in and help the
child, and the family if, God forbid,
anything should ever happen to their
parents.

● ● ● ● ●

Asked to become a vital part of the
child's extended family—like a special
aunt or uncle. For instance, godparents
oftentimes play an important role in the
wedding ceremony if their godchild
gets married.

● ● ● ● ●

One of the most important spiritual
influences in the life of their godchild.

A <u>Great</u> Godparent Can Make an Eternal Difference

We recently asked several teenagers to describe what sort of role their godparents played in their lives. Each of these kids had godparents at their Baptisms. These are some of the answers we received:

● ● ● I have four godparents. Two of them have barely been involved in my life at all. One has been there for me on a few occasions. But I do have one godparent who has really been supportive of me my whole life. She has pushed me to become a better version of myself, and has supported me in the difficult decisions I've had to make. She treats me like I know she would treat her own kids.

● ● ● When one of my parents couldn't be there for me, my godparent was there. It feels as if she can say anything to me, and I feel pretty free to talk to her about anything as well.

● ● ● My godmother has been very helpful at some difficult times in my life. She is very honest with me, willing to talk a lot, and always gives me spiritual books. My other godmother is like that, too. I know my godfather knows me well too, and he has also been helpful.

● ● ● I think the main responsibilities of a godparent are to steer the child to God in their life by talking, giving advice, maybe praying for me, and being an example.

● ● ● My godparents care a lot about me and what I am doing. They do many things with me and have pushed me to find out more about myself and to get closer to Jesus.

● ● ● I think the responsibilities of a godparent are to stay connected with the child and to support them and give them direction, especially if the child can't or would prefer not to go to their parents in a situation. They can also be someone who the child can go to in a time of need or struggling.

● ● ● Sadly, none of my godparents have really had an impact on my life. Two of them were involved with me early on, but I haven't spoken to them for years. The other two haven't really had an influence on my life at all.

● ● ● I think that godparents are supposed to be there to help the godchild through difficulties in their spiritual life and normal life. They are supposed to be there, so the godchild feels like there is someone else looking out for them, other than their parents. They are supposed to be the unrelated parents who care, look out for, and guide the godchild through the difficulties in life. They are supposed to be the people who love the child enough to help them through difficulties that the parents might not be able to help them with.

● ● ● In my life, there are more people who aren't my godparents who actually care for me. They are doing the job that my godparents aren't actually doing. They are helping me make decisions, caring for me, and loving me the way my godparents should.

How interesting these answers are! Consider some of the essentials of what these teenagers, now young women and men, each of whom had experiences with godparents, told us:

" She has pushed me to become a better version of myself.**"**

" It feels as if she can say anything to me, and I feel pretty free to talk to her about anything as well. "

" My godparents care a lot about me and… have pushed me to find out more about myself and to get closer to Jesus. "

" A godparent…can be someone who the child can go to in a time of need or struggling. "

" Godparents are supposed to be the unrelated parents who care, look out for, and guide the godchild through the difficulties in life. "

" They are supposed to be the people who love the child enough to help them through difficulties that the parents might not be able to help them with. "

Great Godparenting Does Not Happen Accidentally

Every godchild wants great godparents, and every godparent has the ability to do great things in the life of their godchild. All it requires is God's grace and your own, personal dedication. And prayer. Try beginning right here and now, with this:

Loving Lord God,

I pray today that you will guide, inspire,

and support me in my role as godparent

to _____.

Shine your divine presence in my life

in new ways, enlighten me with your

wisdom, and show me how to best

reflect your love.

Help me to be a good example of

Christian love and care in the world

around me.

And make me mindful of the needs of

my precious godchild, _____.

Amen.

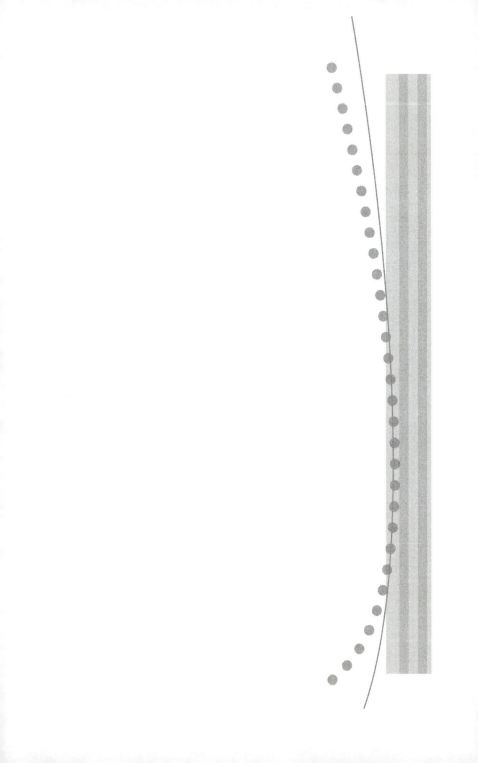

A (Very) Brief History of Christian Godparenting

Jewish Roots

As is the case with many Christian spiritual practices, we mostly inherited this one from ancient Judaism. Have you ever been to a *bris*? After a Jewish boy is born, a sacred ritual is performed known as the *brit milah*, which transliterated from Hebrew means "covenant of circumcision." This is often shorthanded to *bris*, which is a Yiddish word that means, "covenant."

The origins of the *brit milah* are found in the Torah, the first five books of the Bible, written long before the coming of Christ. In the seventeenth chapter of Genesis, God said to Abraham:

This is my covenant, which you shall keep, between me and you and your offspring after you: Every male among you shall be circumcised. You shall circumcise the flesh of your foreskins, and it shall be a sign of the covenant between me and you. Throughout your generations every male among you shall be circumcised when he is eight days old, including the slave born in your house and the one bought with your money from any foreigner who is not of your offspring. Both the slave born in your house and the one bought with your money must be circumcised. So shall my covenant be in your flesh an everlasting covenant. Any uncircumcised male who is not circumcised in the flesh of his foreskin shall be cut off from his people; he has broken my covenant. (Gen. 17:10–14)

Later, God told Moses to instruct the people of
Israel further, adding:

> If a woman conceives and bears a male
> child.... On the eighth day the flesh of his
> foreskin shall be circumcised.
> (Lev. 12:2–3)

The most important reason observant
Jews still perform this ancient ritual on their
sons is simply that God commanded them to
do it. But the spiritual meaning is deeper: the
spiritual meaning of the *brit milah* is that it
unites a boy with his people, Israel; and even
more personally, circumcision itself is a symbol
of how both body and soul are united together
in serving God. It is at this special ceremony,
on the eighth day of the child's life, when the
parents announce to their family and friends the
child's name. His identity as a son of Israel, as a
child of God, begins at his *bris*.

The first Christians inherited this ceremony from Judaism because the first Christians were Jews. They were followers of Christ (Christians) who were Jewish, practicing Jewish rituals and maintaining their Jewish identity. Soon, however, there were other Christians who were non-Jews, or Gentiles, and they had no desire to follow Jewish ritual practice. There followed some serious theological discussion between Peter and Paul in the early years after Christ's resurrection as to whether or not all followers of Christ, going forward, needed to be circumcised. (See Acts 15 and Galatians 2:11–21 for passages in the Bible that discuss this.) In the end, at an event known in history as The Jerusalem Conference in the year AD 50, a gathering of Christian leaders including Peter and Paul decided it was unnecessary to be Jewish in order to be this new creation: a Christian.

Still, ancient Judaism permeates many Christian spiritual practices.

At every *bris*, there is a *sandek*, which is another Hebrew word meaning "companion of a child." This is an adult, a close friend of the family, who is charged with the honor of handing the infant into the hands of his father, or who holds the boy in his arms during the circumcision. This person is called upon to support the parents, emotionally and spiritually, as well. The *sandek* is supposed to be a person of deep piety. The ancient rabbis compared the *sandek* to the altar in the Temple. In fact, in ancient texts, the Jewish sages teach that the spiritual qualities of a *sandek* are somehow mystically transferred to the child.

This is the rich historical context for having sponsors at a child's Baptism. There was always a sponsor (*sandek*) for a Jewish boy at his *brit milah*, and so, too, there would be sponsors, or godparents, for the children of Christian Baptism.

Over time, many differences developed between the two practices. We will not mention them all here, but by way of example, being asked to be a *sandek* is often an honor given to the child's paternal or maternal grandfather; whereas in Christianity, baptismal sponsors are usually chosen from among lifelong friends outside of the family, not from among direct family members. Also, a *sandek* has no responsibility for educating the child in Judaism after the *bris* is over. A godparent has responsibility for both the religious education and spiritual formation of their godchild after Baptism.

A Sacrament

Baptism has always been primarily about welcoming new members into the Christian community. It is also what we call a "sacrament." There is this beautiful sentence in the *Catechism of the Catholic Church* on the meaning of all of the sacraments, including Baptism:

> Sacraments are efficacious signs of
> grace, instituted by Christ and entrusted

to the Church, by which divine life is
dispensed to us. [n. 1131]

Jesus Christ instituted Baptism, as we read
in the Gospels; and Baptism—like each of the
sacraments—is one of the primary ways we come
to know God directly, in this life.

Do you remember the story and scene of
Jesus's Baptism by John the Baptist in the Jordan
River? You may want to remind yourself by
finding Luke chapter 3 and reading it carefully.
This is the first time in the Bible that we hear
the name Pontius Pilate. It was when he had
become governor of Judea that "the word of
God came to John son of Zechariah in the
wilderness" (Luke 3:2). The Gospel writer
compares John the Baptist to the prophet Isaiah,
as one who "prepares the way of the Lord." And
Jesus clearly understands his cousin John to be
that kind of prophet, too, because while John
is preaching to the crowds and baptizing all

who come to him, Jesus approaches and offers himself for Baptism.

But…wait a minute! How could John the Baptist be performing a sacrament that Jesus had not yet instituted, yet alone undergone? The answer is simple. John the Baptist, like Jesus, was a Jew, and this is again where we see the Jewish origins of Christian practice. What John was doing was understood to be Baptism by the time Luke wrote his Gospel. But the Jewish people coming to John in that wilderness considered it to be what they called a *mikveh*, or a ritual bath in natural, flowing water, in order to obtain purity—or holiness before God. All Jews were encouraged to enter a *mikveh* from time to time in order to renew their spiritual commitments. And converts to the Jewish faith always entered a *mikveh* as a public representation of their commitment and change in status.

The Gospels were written in ancient Greek (not the Hebrew of Judaism and the Old Testament). And the word "Baptism" is from a Greek noun, *baptismos,* and means simply, "washing." So, as the Gospel of Luke tells us, John was truly "preparing the way of the Lord" (Luke 3:4).

In the New Testament and Ancient Church

Most of the first Baptisms we read about in the New Testament involved adult converts, rather than babies. In those earliest days of the faith, it was assumed that candidates for Baptism would be knowledgeable about the teachings of Christianity, and would have fully accepted them as their own. That is, after all, the reason they were presenting themselves for Baptism in the first place.

But by the second century, infant Baptism became common. As converts were welcomed into the fold, so too were their families. And the parents, extended family, and congregation were asked to make vows promising to assist all in the teaching and transition of faith. This is when godparents first became common—and necessary. Godparents were needed to stand beside the parents and confirm the family's commitment to the confession of faith.

Throughout the ancient church, godparents were recognized as essential for the family, as well as for the child being baptized, and by extension, for the Church itself.

Christianity was illegal in the Roman Empire at this time. Christians were afraid of persecution and being baptized was a bold stand to take. Sometimes a new Christian would face martyrdom for her faith at the hands of the Roman authorities before she was able to undergo the rite of Baptism. This became so common in the third century that martyrdom itself came to be called "Baptism by blood."

There was also a fear in the early church of pagans entering the faith and watering down its core principles and beliefs. During certain eras there were so many converts joining at such a rapid pace, that, although they were welcomed when their conversion was sincere, the first religious educators wanted to be sure they were adequately instructed. Early catechesis, therefore, made godparents essential! Each godparent—or "sponsor" at a Baptism—played the important role of verifying the sincerity of the convert, whether it be the child (or adult), or the family in which that child was raised.

Early theologians and bishops often referred to godparents as "spiritual fathers and mothers" to their godchildren, and even as "spiritual co-parents," because their role was so important. This is the ideal that we should aspire to, even and especially today, in our own godparenting.

CHAPTER THREE

Who Can Be a Godparent?

According to the Code of Canon Law of the Catholic Church (Canon 874), not everyone is able to be a godparent. The Church offers specific guidelines, and your local parish priest will help you understand them. In preparation, take a few moments now to consider these guidelines carefully.

Note that the terms "godparent" and "sponsor" are not always interchangeable. A "godparent" is a person who fulfills all of the lifetime responsibilities implied by that title; and a "sponsor" is a specific responsibility—usually of the godparents—at a child's Baptism.

First, Canon 874 reads that a godparent must:

"Be appointed by the candidate for Baptism, or by the parents or whoever stands in their place, or failing these, by the parish priest or the minister."

"Be suitable for this role and have the intention of fulfilling it."

"Be not less than sixteen years of age, unless a different age has been stipulated by the diocesan bishop, or unless the parish priest or the minister considers that there is a just reason for an exception to be made."

"Be a Catholic who has been confirmed and has received the blessed Eucharist, and who lives a life of faith which befits the role to be undertaken."

"Not labor under a canonical penalty, whether imposed or declared."

"Not be either the father or the mother of the person to be baptized."

Finally, provision is made whereby a non-Catholic Christian may act as godparent to a Catholic child. The Canon states that "a baptized person who belongs to a non-Catholic ecclesial community may be" a godparent, in cases where there is also a Catholic sponsor. In such instances—and this is where the distinction between "godparenting" and "sponsoring" comes into play—the non-Catholic godparent acts as a "witness," rather than as an official "sponsor," at the Baptism.

If you have any questions about these guidelines, be sure to discuss them with your parish priest.

CHAPTER FOUR

A
Spiritual
Companion

In chapter one, we outlined six essential things that every great godparent should do. Let's now look at each of these in detail.

Godparents are physically present as sponsors, and thoughtfully and prayerfully involved on the occasion of the child's Baptism; and then later, for his or her confirmation.

Your responsibilities begin at the child's Baptism. Each of us becomes a member of the Catholic Church when we are baptized. Baptism is the first of three sacraments that initiate us in the Catholic faith. The other two are Confirmation and the Holy Eucharist, or Holy Communion. Each of these sacraments was instituted by our Lord Jesus Christ himself.

The Importance of a Child's Baptism

It is through Baptism that we are truly and formally brought into the family of God. Through this sacrament, we each become a "child of God."

About the waters of Baptism: Every sacrament involves the use of what we call a sacramental. These are material items set apart, or made holy, and then used in conjunction with a sacrament in order to make that sacrament most meaningful to us. Each of us is baptized with the sacramental of blessed holy water, but just as literally by God the Holy Spirit, as we take upon ourselves the responsibility of becoming a member of God's family.

The baptismal font is most often located in one of two places in the church: near the entrance, emphasizing that Baptism is the beginning of a Christian life; or near the sanctuary, close to the altar, emphasizing how what begins in Baptism is celebrated and completed in our lives through the Holy Eucharist.

Sponsors stand beside the family and the child at an infant Baptism, beginning the long and important journey of helping both family and child develop a great appreciation for the faith. For parents to have a child baptized in the Church means they are accepting the responsibility of training their child in the practice of the faith. And, as a godparent/ sponsor, you are a companion in faith. It is the duty of both parents and godparents/sponsors to bring up a child to keep God's commandments as Christ taught us, by loving God and our neighbor. This is a tremendous responsibility and demands a great deal of commitment.

The best way to teach children is always by example. Your words and your example will be your most important contribution to the spiritual formation of your godchild. This starts at the child's Baptism. Later, in Confirmation, we receive the fullness of God's Spirit and take on the responsibility to live our faith by our own choice. And, in the sacrament of Holy Communion we share at the banquet of Christ's sacrifice, calling God our Father in the midst of the Church and deepening our relationship with God and the whole community. These two sacraments cannot happen, and cannot bless our lives and those of the Church, without our first being baptized and initiated into the people of God.

During the Divine Service Itself

Baptisms almost always take place in church on Sundays, at the same time that the Holy Eucharist is celebrated. The baptismal rite begins with the parents and the godparents "presenting" the child to the parish for Holy Baptism. The celebrant or priest takes the child in his arms and says, "What name do you give [or have you given] your child?"

The parents then respond with the baptismal name, and the priest continues, "What do you ask of God's Church for him / her?" And the parents say "Holy Baptism" or "Eternal life" or another phrase that means the holy, eternal faith and grace of Christ that comes only through Baptism.

Then the priest or celebrant speaks to the parents, reminding them of their responsibility to bring up the child as Christ has taught us. He finishes by saying, "Do you understand what you are undertaking?"

The parents respond: "I do."

Then the priest or celebrant turns to the godparents and says the same to them. This is where you need to be ready to answer! He will finish by saying something like, "Are you ready to help the parents of [name] with this undertaking?"

The godparents respond: "I am."

Then the priest or celebrant proclaims that the Christian community welcomes the child with joy and says, "I claim you for Christ our Savior by the sign of his cross," as he traces the cross on the child's forehead, and then asks parents (and usually the godparents) to do the same. After this comes the Celebration of the Word, when Holy Scripture is read, and a homily is preached. The priest will often invite the parents, godparents, and other family members to participate in this part of the service as well.

Next are the Intercessions, or prayers for the child being baptized.

This is followed by the Prayer of Exorcism and Anointing. This is the most misunderstood portion of the service. Simply put, the Church believes that evil and Satan are real and active in the world, but that Christ always conquers evil with love. The priest or celebrant prays the prayer of exorcism, which usually is something like this: "Almighty and ever-living God, you sent your only Son into the world to cast out the power of Satan, the spirit of evil, to rescue man from the kingdom of darkness, and bring him into the splendor of your kingdom of light. We pray for this child: set [name] free from original sin, make him/her a temple of your glory, and send your Holy Spirit to dwell with him/her. We ask this through Christ our Lord." The congregation says, "Amen."

Then the priest or celebrant says: "We anoint you with the oil of salvation in the name of Christ our Savior; may he strengthen you with his power, who lives and reigns forever and ever." And the congregation says, "Amen."

Then the priest or celebrant, the parents and godparents, and the child all move to the baptismal font. There, the priest blesses the water, turning it from ordinary water into the water of resurrection in Christ. The celebrant then questions the parents and godparents. He says, "Do you reject Satan?"

Parents and Godparents: "I do." (Not "*We* do." Speak only for yourself.)

"And all his works?"

"I do."

"Do you reject sin, so as to live in the freedom of God's children?"

"I do."

"Do you reject the glamour of evil, and refuse to be mastered by sin?"

"I do."

"Do you reject Satan, father of sin and prince of darkness?"

"I do."

"Do you believe in God, the Father almighty, creator of heaven and earth?"

"I do."

"Do you believe in Jesus Christ, his only Son, our Lord, who was born of the Virgin Mary, was crucified, died, and was buried, rose from the dead, and is now seated at the right hand of the Father?"

"I do."

"Do you believe in the Holy Spirit, the holy catholic Church, the communion of saints, the forgiveness of sins, the resurrection of the body, and life everlasting?"

"I do."

Then, the congregation is asked to confirm its commitment to these principles of faith as well.

At this point, the rest of the family gathers around the font with you, if they hadn't already. The priest continues by asking the parents and the godparents: "Is it your will that [name] should be baptized in the faith of the Church, which we have all professed with you?"

"It is." And then he baptizes the child, saying: "[Name], I baptize you in the name of the Father, (while immersing the child or pouring water on his/her head), and of the Son (repeating), and of the Holy Spirit (repeating)."

How to Help Create Lasting Memories

Your responsibilities begin at the child's Baptism, but they don't end there. How will you "stay in touch," especially if you are not fortunate enough to live near your godchild?

MEANINGFUL GIFT IDEAS

- Books or prayer cards on a favorite saint, or the child's patron saint

- Age-appropriate Bible

- Rosary

- Engraved picture frame

- Painting or cross to hang in the child's room

- Framed print detailing the meaning of the child's name

- Special jewelry with religious significance, such as a cross or angel

- "Keepsake box" for special mementos as the child grows up

- Framed photo of you with your godchild

Many godparents will do this by sending their godchild a special card every year to mark the occasion of his or her Baptism anniversary. It is good to remind ourselves that the occasion of our Baptism is just as important, if not more, than our birthday. You were born on your birthday, but you were born into God's family on the day of your Baptism.

If you live near your godchild, of course, not only can you send a card, but also you can visit and mark the occasion in other, special ways.

Godparents are physically present at other important moments in the child's life as he or she grows into adulthood. If the child lives nearby, this is simple. But even if he or she lives far away, godparents need to make an effort to see the child frequently.

It is a misconception that a godparent is primarily a gift-giver. This was not the intention of the early Church fathers when they established the role of godparents/sponsors in the Sacrament of Baptism. In fact, in the past there have been some parents who mistakenly selected friends of the family who were financially well-off while, perhaps, less gifted spiritually. That mistake is rarely made today. We have learned how important it is for the godparent to be a spiritual mentor.

For all of these reasons, keep in mind that giving—or sending—gifts is of course fine, but not at all a primary function of a godparent. When you want to send a gift, consider educational and inspirational gifts rather than toys or entertainment. For example, many parishes where kids are confirmed in high school will give each child a *Catholic Youth Bible* to use during their course of study. This resource can be invaluable for answering common questions and encouraging a love of reading Holy Scripture. You may also want to select books for your godchild that explain essential religious topics such as the Church, prayer, holiness, the Trinity, the Blessed Virgin Mary, Sacred Scripture, the Ten Commandments, the Beatitudes, and the Sacraments.

> Godparents are there to help guide
> the spiritual formation and religious
> education of the child.

Many godparents report that they spend time on their knees every day, and at Mass regularly, praying for the spiritual needs of their godchild. Other godparents study the Bible on the subject of how to raise a child as a faithful Christian. There are many proverbs, psalms, and stories that are relevant to raising—and helping to spiritually guide—children to become men and women of real faith. You may want to turn to verses such as these. Consider, in fact, committing some to memory— or writing/printing them out and sticking them

to the front of your refrigerator beside a photo of
your godchild.

> With my whole heart I seek you;
>
> do not let me stray from your
>
> commandments.
>
> I treasure your word in my heart,
>
> so that I may not sin against you.
>
> Blessed are you, O LORD;
>
> teach me your statutes.
>
> (Psalm 119:10–12)

> Josiah was eight years old when he
>
> began to reign; he reigned for thirty-one
>
> years in Jerusalem. He did what was
>
> right in the sight of the LORD, and walked
>
> in the ways of his ancestor David; he did
>
> not turn aside to the right or to the left.
>
> (2 Chronicles 34:1–2)

[Jesus] called a child, whom he put among them, and said, "Truly I tell you, unless you change and become like children, you will never enter the kingdom of heaven. Whoever becomes humble like this child is the greatest in the kingdom of heaven." (Matthew 18:2–4)

People were bringing little children to him in order that he might touch them; and the disciples spoke sternly to them. But when Jesus saw this, he was indignant and said to them, "Let the little children come to me; do not stop them; for it is to such as these that the kingdom of God belongs. Truly I tell you, whoever does not receive the kingdom of God as a little child will never enter it." And he took them up in his arms, laid his hands on them, and blessed them. (Mark 10:13–16)

> Children, obey your parents in the Lord,
> for this is right. "Honor your father and
> mother"—this is the first commandment
> with a promise: "so that it may be well
> with you and you may live long on the
> earth." (Ephesians 6:1–3)

Talk with your godchild, as well, about the history of the Church, how to begin to understand the meaning of Holy Scripture, and the most essential ways of living a moral life according to Catholic principles. For this last category—living a moral life—you may want to take some time yourself to study Blessed Pope John Paul II's two encyclicals *Veritatis splendor* and *Fides et ratio*. In the Introduction to *Veritatis splendor*, the Pope wrote these inspiring summaries and challenges:

> Called to salvation through faith in Jesus
> Christ, "the true light that enlightens
> everyone" (John 1:9), people become

"light in the Lord" and "children of light"
(Ephesians 5:8), and are made holy by
"obedience to the truth" (1 Peter 1:22).

This obedience is not always easy. As
a result of that mysterious original sin,
committed at the prompting of Satan,
the one who is "a liar and the father
of lies" (John 8:44), man is constantly
tempted to turn his gaze away from the
living and true God in order to direct it
towards idols (cf. 1 Thessalonians 1:9),
exchanging "the truth about God for a
lie" (Romans 1:25).

No one can escape from the
fundamental questions: *What must I do?*
How do I distinguish good from evil?
The answer is only possible thanks to
the splendor of the truth which shines
forth deep within the human spirit, as the

Psalmist bears witness: "There are many who say: 'O that we might see some good! Let the light of your face shine on us, O LORD.'" (Psalm 4:6)

The Church knows that the issue of morality is one which deeply touches every person; it involves all people, even those who do not know Christ and his Gospel or God himself. She knows that it is precisely *on the path of the moral life that the way of salvation is open to all.*[1]

Hopefully, this will whet your appetite to discover, in Scripture, together with your godchild, what it means to answer the most fundamental questions of life, as a Catholic.

---

1 *Veritatis splendor,* encyclical of Blessed Pope John Paul II, August 5, 1993; Introduction, paragraphs 1, 2, and 3. The entire text is available in English on the Vatican website, at http://www.vatican.va/holy_father/john_paul_ii /encyclicals/documents/hf_jp-ii_enc_06081993_veritatis-splendor_en.html.

Godparents are prepared to step in and help the child, and the family if, God forbid, anything should ever happen to their parents.

This principle of godparenting emphasizes that this is a lifetime commitment. As we have stated, your responsibilities involve far more than simply being present at the child's Baptism. You need to remain involved in his or her life for as long as you live. God has blessed you with this new, lifelong relationship—indeed, for eternity!

There are times when, sadly, this provision of being a godparent comes into play. In the "old countries" in earlier centuries, it was a matter of due course for the godparent to raise the child, rather than send the child to an orphanage, if the parents died. But of course, today there is no legal commitment on the part of godparents to raise their godchildren after the death of the parents, unless it was formally agreed upon and written in the parents' will. Simply becoming a godparent does not imply raising the children under such circumstances. But your friends, the child's parents, may wish to formalize your role in their lives in this way and you should be prepared to discuss the possibility. Alternatively, if you or they choose for whatever reason to appoint someone else as guardian of the child, in the case of the parents' death, you as godparent should be aware of who that is—because your relationship with the child continues forever.

Godparents are asked to become a
vital part of the extended family—like
a special aunt or uncle. For instance,
godparents often play an important
role in the wedding ceremony if their
godchild gets married.

Some parents will deliberately not choose
members of the extended family as their child's
godparents. This is because family members
already enjoy and undertake the close relationship
responsibilities that are also expected of godparents.
So, godparents outside of the family are like adding
new, additional aunts and uncles!

However, there have been millions of great
godparents among family members over the
centuries. The measure of success is up to you as
godparent. How committed will you be?

By the time your godchild reaches marriageable
age, you will have been to dozens of birthday
parties, soccer games, his or her First Communion,

Confirmation, high school graduation, and perhaps even college graduation, and beyond. You will be like an aunt or uncle to the child, as close as family. How natural, then, that you would play an important role in getting to know his or her future spouse, and then, in the wedding ceremony itself. (Sometimes a godparent will even offer to help the parents pay for the wedding by footing the cost of the photographer, or the flowers, or some other not insignificant item.)

A Blessing for My Godchild on Her/His Wedding Day

I thank you, loving God, for the affection

that you long ago planted in my heart,

and for the many blessings I have

experienced loving my goddaughter/

godson, _____.

Now, on this miraculous day,

she/he has vowed to love

_____ for eternity.

I thank you again for your blessings.

It is you who brought these two together.

Bless their marriage, O God,

with peace and happiness and house

full of love and faithfulness to you and

your Church, and may we all be blessed

by being a part of their lives.

I know that I have been!

Amen.

> Godparents are one of the most
> important spiritual influences in the life
> of their godchild!

How will you be a spiritual influence on your godchild? This is the most important task of all.

Above all else, you need to be available to your goddaughter or godson. There are many ways that you can do this, especially if you live nearby. Godparents often sit with their godchild at Mass. They often offer to personally take their godchild to Mass on those occasions when the parents are unable to do so.

But even more important than being present, is being a holy example. As the Bible says, "a person is justified by works and not by faith alone" (James 2:24). This is the most basic and essential point of all: Godparents embody the faith to their godchildren—by example. This means being willing to share your faith, and showing through your daily life, actions, and decisions that you make Jesus Christ your way, your truth, and your life. (See John 14:6.)

All Christians are supposed to follow these words of admonition in the Bible: "Show yourself in all respects a model of good works, and in your teaching show integrity" (Titus 2:7). But then those who lead and teach others are especially advised to be careful of their moral example. As it says in the Book of James:

> Not many of you should become teachers, my brothers and sisters, for you know that we who teach will be judged with greater strictness. For all of us make many mistakes. Anyone who makes no mistakes in speaking is perfect, able to keep the whole body in check with a bridle. If we put bits into the mouths of horses to make them obey us, we guide their whole bodies. Or look at ships: though they are so large that it

takes strong winds to drive them, yet
they are guided by a very small rudder
wherever the will of the pilot directs. So
also the tongue is a small member, yet
it boasts of great exploits. How great a
forest is set ablaze by a small fire!...

Who is wise and understanding among
you? Show by your good life that your
works are done with gentleness born
of wisdom. But if you have bitter envy
and selfish ambition in your hearts,
do not be boastful and false to the
truth. Such wisdom does not come
down from above, but is earthly,
unspiritual, devilish. For where there
is envy and selfish ambition, there
will also be disorder and wickedness
of every kind. But the wisdom from
above is first pure, then peaceable,
gentle, willing to yield, full of mercy

and good fruits, without a trace of partiality or hypocrisy. And a harvest of righteousness is sown in peace for those who make peace.

(James 3:1–5, 13–18)

WAYS TO SUPPORT YOUR GODCHILD

- Celebrate the anniversary of their holy day of Baptism with a visit, a call, or a card.
- As your godchild grows, be available to listen and share in the struggles and joys of the Christian life.
- Encourage a growing life of faith, welcoming honest conversation and relationship.
- Be involved as your godchild receives the other sacraments.
- Be supportive of your godchild's parents as they guide their child in the Christian faith.

- Be present (if possible) and emotionally involved in important milestones in your godchild's life, such as birthdays and graduations.
- Support your godchild's unique interests and gifts, as they discover God's call on their life.
- Become a trusted friend and mentor as they grow older and navigate their way through life.
- Most importantly, become an example of wholehearted Christian living for your godchild.

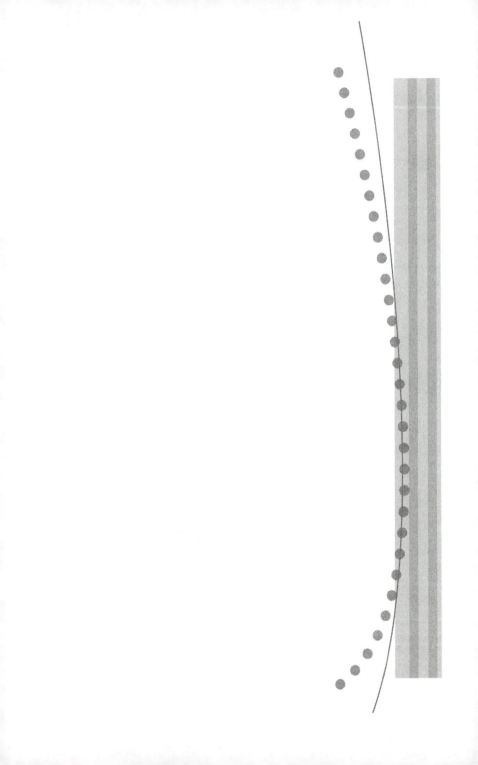

CHAPTER FIVE

The Whole Parish as Godparent

As we have seen, godparents play an important role in the lives of their godchildren, but the entire parish has responsibilities, too, for the religious education, spiritual development, and growth in faith of your godchild. It is worth taking a few minutes to think about this.

If you wanted a child to learn his multiplication tables, it is conceivable that you could buy him a book that explains them thoroughly, and entrust a single teacher to explain them and then drill them into his memory. That might work.

Now, imagine that you wanted a child to learn how to love others, or to love God. Could you purchase a book that tells about how to do those things, ask her to read it, and leave her with a single teacher to help drive home the most salient points? Would you expect the child to grow up knowing how to love God and her neighbor? Probably not. Some things are more complicated—and dare we say, more important!—than multiplication tables. The Christian life is surely more important—in fact, about as important as anything on earth.

It takes a whole parish to raise a godchild. You will have plenty of help.

Be sure to always look to priests and educators for help and advice. Discuss with parish counselors and confessors, and also professionals outside the Church when necessary, matters of concern you have for your godchild.

If you remain within the loving arms of the Church, you will find that there are people all around you willing, able, and wanting to help your godchild grow in Christ.

CHAPTER SIX

Prayers and
Blessings
for You
and Your Godchild

● FOR GODPARENTS

The Prayer of Every Godparent

Loving Lord God,

Who creates and sustains all things,

Make your blessings known to me today,

And fill my heart with gratitude for all that you have

done in my life.

Today, I bring before you _____,

My beloved godchild.

Guard and protect him/her.

Show me how best to love and care for him/her.

And guide and support me as I walk the road of

salvation beside him/her.

Give me your words, your wisdom, and your love.
Help me to be an example of Christ in his/her life.
Amen.

A Prayer of St. Thomas Aquinas

Give us, O Lord, a steadfast heart,
One that no unworthy attentions can
drag downward.
Give us a heart without fear,
That no tribulation can wear out.
Give us a pure heart,
So that no unholy purpose may tempt
us away.
And give us also, O Lord our God,
Understanding to know you,
Diligence to seek you,
Wisdom to find you,
And a faithfulness that may finally
embrace you,
Through Jesus Christ our Lord.

Prayer for the Relationship between Godchild and Godparent

Loving God, today we mark the occasion of a wonderful relationship that has its beginning in you.

Thank you for _____

and _____.

May they grow together to know your love, your mercy, and your salvation beginning this day and for evermore.

Bless and guide them; may they be the best of friends, reminding the world around them of your love.

Amen.

● FOR GODCHILDREN, LOOKING BACK A FEW YEARS LATER

My Baptism

A prayer poem for children by Patricia Clough

Today I took a closer step

to be with Heavenly Father.

I humbly walked down five white steps

and into clean, clear water.

My loving Daddy took my hand

to help me stand up straight—

Just as he has through all my life

till now when I am eight.

My Daddy showed me what to do—

breathe deep and hold your nose—

And baptized me with priesthood power

and smiled when I arose.

Tomorrow I'll take another step

to be with Heavenly Father.

My Daddy, uncles, grandpas too,

will all around me gather.

They'll lay their hands upon my head,

bless me and say, "Amen."

Then the Holy Ghost will be my guide

if I but follow Him.

My Gift

What can I give Him

Poor as I am;

If I were a shepherd,

I would give Him a lamb.

If I were a wise man,

I would do my part.

But what can I give Him?

I will give him my heart.

—Christina Rossetti

● FOR GODPARENTS TO RECITE TO THEIR GODCHILDREN

The Priestly Blessing from the Bible

The LORD bless you and keep you;

the LORD make his face to shine upon

you, and be gracious to you;

the LORD lift up his countenance upon

you, and give you peace.

—Numbers 6:24–26

May God Bless My Godchild

Loving God of power and glory, I thank you today for my godchild _____. He/she is your beloved child, in whom you are well pleased, and you know every hair on his/her head. Guard and protect him/her. Watch over him/her, and keep him/her walking in your ways all the days of her/his life. May the Lord God bless you, my godchild, _____, and me, too, as we journey together in the love of Christ. Amen.

A Prayer of Gratitude

Dear Heavenly Father,
Thank you for the gift of _____
and for all the joy that he/she brings to our lives.
Please be with her/him on her/his Christian journey,
showing each of us how to support and

guide her/him along the way,

so that she/he may come to know our

Lord Jesus Christ

more and more each day,

as Savior, as Shepherd, as Friend. Amen.

● PRAYERS AND SCRIPTURE FOR CHILDREN TO LEARN

Psalm 23 (NKJV)

The LORD *is* my shepherd; I shall not want.

He makes me to lie down in green pastures;

He leads me beside the still waters.

He restores my soul;

He leads me in the paths of righteousness

For His name's sake.

Yea, though I walk through the valley of the

shadow of death,

I will fear no evil;

For You *are* with me;

Your rod and Your staff, they comfort me.

You prepare a table before me in the

presence of my enemies;

You anoint my head with oil;

My cup runs over.

Surely goodness and mercy shall follow me

All the days of my life;

And I will dwell in the house of the LORD

Forever.

Our Father

Our Father who art in heaven,

hallowed be Thy name;

Thy Kingdom come;

Thy will be done

on earth as it is in heaven.

Give us this day our daily bread;

and forgive us our trespasses

as we forgive those who trespass

against us;

and lead us not into temptation,

but deliver us from evil. Amen.

The Glory Be

Glory be to the Father,

and to the Son,

and to the Holy Spirit.

As it was in the beginning,

is now, and ever shall be,

world without end.

Amen.

The Act of Contrition

O my God, I am heartily sorry for having

offended Thee, and I detest all my sins,

because I dread the loss of Heaven, and

the pains of Hell; but most of all because

I love Thee, my God, Who art all good

and deserving of all my love. I firmly

resolve, with the help of Thy grace, to

confess my sins, to do penance, and to

amend my life. Amen.

Prayer to the Holy Spirit

Come, Holy Spirit, fill the hearts of your
faithful.

And kindle in them the fire of your love.

Send forth your Spirit and they shall be
created.

And you will renew the face of the earth.

Lord, by the light of the Holy Spirit

you have taught the hearts of your faithful.

In the same Spirit

help us to relish what is right

and always rejoice in your consolation.

We ask this through Christ our Lord.

Amen.

Mark 16:16

The one who believes and is baptized
will be saved.

Titus 3:5–7

He saved us, not because of any works
of righteousness that we had done,
but according to his mercy, through
the water of rebirth and renewal by the
Holy Spirit. This Spirit he poured out
on us richly through Jesus Christ our
Savior, so that, having been justified
by his grace, we might become heirs
according to the hope of eternal life.

My Guardian Angel

Angel of God, my holy guardian dear,
to whom God's love entrusts me here,
ever this day [or night] be at my side
to light and guard, to rule and guide.
Amen.

CHAPTER SEVEN

Four Commonly Asked Questions

You may still have a lot of questions about how to be a great godparent. You will receive good advice from many quarters, including your local priest, friends and family, and the Holy Spirit will show you the way as you prayerfully go forward. Be sure to spend regular time with God in prayer, and ask the Spirit to guide you.

In the meantime, you may still have lots of questions.

As we talked with godparents and godchildren, we discovered there were a few basic questions that are asked over and over again. Below are some clear answers to four of those most commonly asked.

What if I disagree with how the parents are raising my godchild? Should I say something? Or, should I not?

The simple answer is: Yes, but be sensitive in the way you do it.

You have been entrusted with the enormous responsibility of helping to mentor and guide the spiritual faith of your godchild. Of course, the parents of that child are the most important spiritual influences on him or her, but after the parents, it's you; so if you have concerns, you should voice them, albeit…gently and sensitively, in a spirit of Christian graciousness, listening, and understanding.

I am a sincere Protestant Christian believer. Why can't I be the godparent to the child of my best friends, who are Catholic?

The Church asks all Catholic parents to choose godparents that are members of the Catholic Church, baptized and confirmed as Catholics. This is because the Church wants to be sure that a child is raised, not only as a faithful Christian, but also as a knowledgeable Catholic. If you are a Catholic in faithful communion with the Church, and confirmed yourself, it is likely that you have already answered many of the questions that your godchild will face, for yourself. That's important. There is a difference between being a faithful Christian and a knowledgeable Catholic—sometimes we do not see the importance of the difference—but in this, which is probably the most important of the sacraments of Catholic faith, the difference matters a great deal to the Church. And, to many Catholics.

Try not to take offense at this. There is certainly none intended! And, by all means, don't blame your Catholic friends for wanting to observe this teaching and tradition by selecting Catholics as godparents for their children. You can and still will have a tremendously important influence on the child of your friends.

What if I have to move away, far from where my godchild lives?

There are no boundaries to family and godparenting. You can be a great godparent from far away. We discussed some of these ways in chapter four. Your prayers, your example, and your teaching are what you have vowed to regularly share with your godchild. That said, however, if you must move away, it would be ideal if you were intentional about returning to visit your godchild periodically and regularly—perhaps at least once each year.

I am concerned about being a
godparent because my own faith does
not seem robust enough for me to be
a "teacher" of anyone else. Does that
mean I should say "no"?

Not necessarily. For thousands of godparents,
the honor of being asked, and then the grace that
allowed them to say "yes," is what led them to
become more intentional about their own faith.
Being a godparent can be a sure way to deepen
your own faith. You may want to consider that as a
possibility, instead of saying no!

ADDITIONAL RESOURCES

The following books, experts, websites, and organizations are listed here because they are excellent places for you to go with your additional questions.

On Baptism in the Church

BOOK: *Everything Is Sacred: An Introduction to the Sacrament of Baptism*, by Thomas Scirghi, SJ (Brewster, MA: Paraclete Press, 2012). Father James Martin calls this "The best book on Baptism I've ever read."

VIDEO/DVD: *The Sacrament of Baptism: A Guide to This Celebration of New Life*, with Thomas Scirghi, SJ, and Pastor John K. Stendahl (Brewster, MA: Paraclete Video, 2013).

On the Moral Life

ENCYCLICALS: *Veritatis splendor*, August 5, 1993; and *Fides et ratio*, September 14, 1998, both by

Blessed Pope John Paul II. The entire text of both encyclicals is available in English on the Vatican website, at http://www.vatican.va/holy_ father/john_paul_ii/encyclicals/index.htm.

Deepening a Life of Prayer

BOOK: *On Prayer: A Letter to My Godchild*, by Phyllis Zagano, (Barnharyt, MO: Liguori Publications, 2001).

BOOK: *A Book of Prayers*, by International Committee on English in the Liturgy, Inc. (ICEL), 1982. Various editions. The English translation of "Prayer to the Holy Spirit," on page 72, is taken from this resource.

BOOK: *Catholic Spiritual Practices: A Treasury of Old and New*, edited by Colleen M. Griffith and Thomas H. Groome (Brewster, MA: Paraclete Press, 2012).

The Teachings of the Church

YOUR LOCAL PRIEST.

BOOK: After your local priest, the best single resource would have to be the *Catechism of the Catholic Church, Second Edition*, available as a print book from any Catholic or general bookseller, and also available online, in an easy-to-navigate format, at the website of the United States Conference of Catholic Bishops' website. See this link: http://www.usccb.org/beliefs-and-teachings /what-we-believe/catechism/catechism-of-the -catholic-church/epub/index.cfm.

ABOUT PARACLETE PRESS

WHO WE ARE

Paraclete Press is a publisher of books, recordings, and DVDs on Christian spirituality. Our publishing represents a full expression of Christian belief and practice—from Catholic to Evangelical, from Protestant to Orthodox.

We are the publishing arm of the Community of Jesus, an ecumenical monastic community in the Benedictine tradition. As such, we are uniquely positioned in the marketplace without connection to a large corporation and with informal relationships to many branches and denominations of faith.

WHAT WE ARE DOING

Books

Paraclete publishes books that show the richness and depth of what it means to be Christian. Although Benedictine spirituality is at the heart of all that we do, we publish books that reflect the Christian experience across many cultures, time periods, and houses of worship. We publish books that nourish the vibrant life of the church and its people—books about spiritual practice, formation, history, ideas, and customs.

We have several different series, including the best-selling Paraclete Essentials and Paraclete Giants series of classic texts in contemporary English; A Voice from the Monastery—men and women monastics writing about living a spiritual life today; award-winning poetry; best-selling gift books for children on the occasions of Baptism and first communion; and the Active Prayer Series that brings creativity and liveliness to any life of prayer.

Recordings

From Gregorian chant to contemporary American choral works, our music recordings celebrate sacred choral music through the centuries. Paraclete distributes the recordings of the internationally acclaimed choir Gloriæ Dei Cantores, praised for their "rapt and fathomless spiritual intensity" by *American Record Guide*, and the Gloriæ Dei Cantores Schola, which specializes in the study and performance of Gregorian chant. Paraclete is also the exclusive North American distributor of the recordings of the Monastic Choir of St. Peter's Abbey in Solesmes, France, long considered to be a leading authority on Gregorian chant.

Videos

Our videos offer spiritual help, healing, and biblical guidance for life issues: grief and loss, marriage, forgiveness, anger management, facing death, and spiritual formation.

Learn more about us at our website:
www.paracletepress.com,
or call us toll-free at 1-800-451-5006.

SCAN
TO
READ
MORE

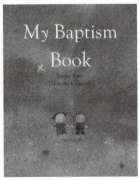

My Baptism Book
Sophie Piper

ISBN: 978-1-55725-535-8
$14.95, Hardcover

Baptism is one of the most important events in a child's life. The message of *My Baptism Book* is one of God's eternal love and care, a perfect Baptism gift for ages 0–8. Gentle, enchanting illustrations bring to life the simple teachings about God, Jesus, and the Holy Spirit that are appropriate for the youngest of children.

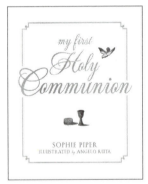

My First Holy Communion
Sophie Piper

ISBN: 978-1-55725-696-6
$14.99, Hardcover

This beautiful book explains the importance of First Communion in language for kids ages 7–9. It includes a variety of blessings and Scripture, and will be welcomed not only as a memento of a special day, but also as an encouragement to grow into maturity as a Christian.